PAPA DOUG HAULS

STRAWBERRIES & SMILES

WORDS BY
Leslie Jones

ILLUSTRATIONS BY
Josh Cassidy

Printed in the United States of America
First Printing, 2014

Illustrator: Josh Cassidy
Author: Leslie Jones

ISBN: 978-0-9916436-0-8

Tennessee Trucking Association
4531 Trousdale Dr., Nashville, TN 37204
www.TNTrucking.org

PAPA DOUG
HAULS
STRAWBERRIES & SMILES

WORDS BY
Leslie Jones

ILLUSTRATIONS BY
Josh Cassidy

Tommy's Papa Doug is a truck driver who spends many nights on the road, driving. But tonight, he'd be home any minute.

Papa's truck takes him everywhere. Tommy imagined Papa driving through outer space and wondered if, someday, Papa would tell him a story about soaring through the solar system.

And just like that, Papa was home.

"Whoa, whoa! You're getting strong — did
a rhino teach you to charge at me like that?
A dinosaur? Or was it a bull from Spain?"

Papa always told the best stories after his time out on the road. Tommy raced to finish his dinner, anticipating tonight's tale.

"What's the rhyme I taught you for tying your shoes, Tom? Can you put a bow in those laces and talk me through it?"

Tommy gave it his best:

"Make a valley, close it up!
Under the mountain one side you'll tuck.
The long road loops around and through …
And together, they bring me back to you."

Papa helped Tommy tidy up his
laces. "Nice work!"

"Are we going somewhere, Papa?"

"You bet! I sit down all day long, and if I don't get some exercise, my legs will shrink. Let's take a walk so that I'm not shorter than you come sundown."

Tommy was in for a treat. Walks with Papa were never just walks — they were adventures.

They started their journey and Papa started his story the way he always had, "Once upon a drive ..."

"It was a busy morning to be on the road. Big, refrigerated trucks like mine, wide loads, motorcycles, flatbeds and four-wheelers — you name it and it was churning down the highway, heading east. Gray clouds covered the sun and sent down raindrops bigger than gumballs."

"My cargo was due early that day, so stopping for the rain wasn't an option, but neither was unsafe driving. See, I have rules to follow just like you do here at home, kiddo."

"What rules, Papa?" Tommy asked.

"Well, one rule says that I can only drive for a certain number of hours per day. Do you know the story of the girl who has to get home before she turns into a pumpkin? I might turn into a frog if I don't stick to my schedule. And then, how would I take care of your mom and you?"

"Another rule says to stop and weigh my truck so I can be sure my cargo hasn't gotten bigger or smaller. And the scale that trucks drive over to weigh themselves is nothing like our bathroom scale. In fact, it's so big that ten elephants, 40 bulls or nearly 500 people could stand on it!"

As Papa paused his story, Tommy noticed they were walking to Smooth Stone Meadow. They had so many fun times there — barrel rolls down the hills in summertime, autumn leaf explorations, sledding in wintertime. It was one of Tommy's favorite places in the whole world.

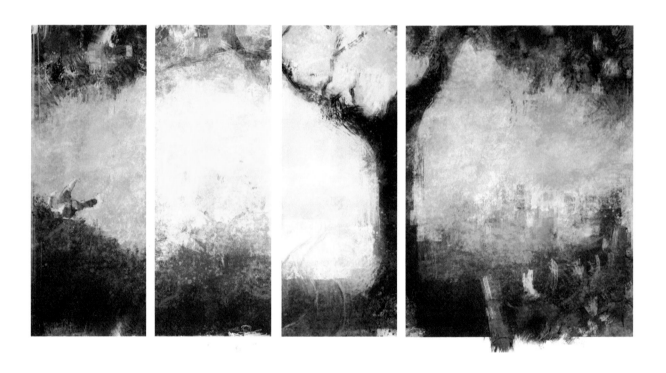

In the spring, the honeysuckle bushes swallowed up the barbed-wire fence, making the whole meadow smell sweet like freshly spun cotton candy.

Up ahead, Tommy saw some of Papa's gardening tools.

"Papa, are we growing a beanstalk?"

"Not today, but maybe someday. Today we're planting reminders."

"Reminders — are those flowers?"

"They're better than flowers. And my story explains why, but you have to be patient. Let's dig some holes and I'll tell you the rest. Whaddaya say?"

"I was still driving in a downpour, just outside of Memphis, Tennessee, on I-40 East, headed toward the small town of Portland, Tennessee. You see, Farmer Mason had called and said Portland's annual strawberry festival was only a few days away and some bad storms had wiped out all of their berries. Lightning and wind took down a whole warehouse full of them, and the heavy rains flooded out the berries still ripening on the vine."

"The strawberry festival is Portland's biggest event all year. And Farmer Mason knew the festival was just what the town needed after such sad, soggy weather.

He was determined they'd have it all right. But there was still one thing missing: fresh strawberries."

"So I decided to help. I picked up a few skids of strawberries from a local farmer in Memphis. My plan was to work a quick stop in Portland into my regular route hauling produce from Memphis to the Great Smoky Mountains.

Trouble was, the weather had different plans."

"The rain still thick, I trudged along in low gear. As I started to pull over and check my weather app, a long line of taillights became clear in the distance. Traffic was still. And right beyond the traffic jam, it looked like the road just … disappeared.

I hissed to a stop and saw that cars were slowly coming through on the other side of the highway. My phone wasn't getting a signal, so I couldn't make calls or see when — or if — a break in the weather was coming. I fired up my CB radio — it works something like your walkie-talkies, letting me talk to other truck drivers nearby. I needed to find out what was happening."

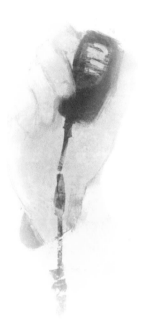

"I flipped to channel 19 on the CB. 'Westbound, this is Eastbound. What's the holdup just outside of the North 40 truck stop?'

A woman's voice came back, 'Copy that, Eastbound 40. A river has flooded over the Eastbound highway. They're rerouting folks back west along the emergency access road in the median, or alternatively onto Highway 641 off Exit 126, just ahead.'

I knew Highway 641 could get me to Portland. It'd be a longer route but higher ground, so I could surely make it. My only choice was to head that way or risk running out of time to save Farmer Mason's festival."

"I waited and waited, inching along while traffic was managed. The day was still gray all around, but all I kept picturing were those ruby-red strawberries and the smiles they'd bring to the people of Portland.

Finally, I started northeast on the new, longer route."

"About an hour outside of Portland,
the clouds broke and the sun started
shining, bright as the day you were born."

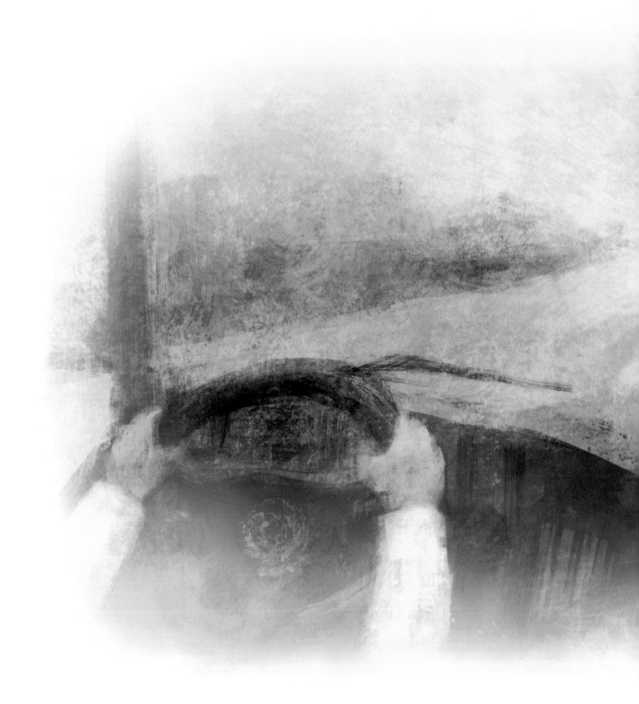

"And before I knew it, I'd made it into town.

'Hooray for strawberries, hooray for Driver Doug!'
the people of Portland shouted.

Seeing their smiles made the longer drive well worth it.
Folks stepped up left and right to fill bowls and bags
with strawberries for preparing their cakes, pies and
goodies for the celebration."

"So the reminders we're planting, Tommy, are strawberry plants. The ones I chose for us are called June bearers, which means that even though we're planting them right now, they may not produce any berries until next summer."

"Next summer? Whoa! That means I'll be seven by the time I eat one! Are they reminders because they'll remind us that they're growing for that long?"

"No, but good guess. Each time we tend to them, they'll remind us that the best things in life — especially some of the smallest, sweetest things — are worth every minute we have to wait for them. And when those simple joys are ripe and right in front of you, you'll know it. You'll know it because you can't help but smile your biggest smile."

And with that, Papa opened a paper bag full of ripe, ruby-red strawberries. As they enjoyed them together, Tommy thought about Papa's words. He knew exactly what Papa meant, because he always smiled the most when Papa was home.

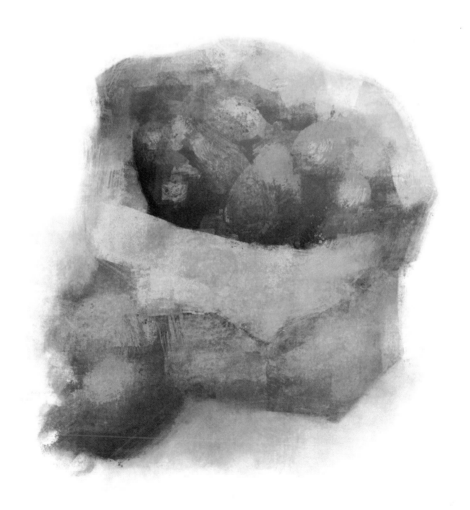

With dirt-stained hands and strawberry-stained smiles,
Tommy and Papa eased home from the meadow,
talking about the colors in the sunset, the stars soon
to shine and strawberry pie.

The End

CPSIA information can be obtained
at www.ICGtesting.com
Printed in the USA
LVIC05n0456051114
412094LV00002B/3